Bee Jokes
Funny Bee Jokes for Kids

Arnie Lightning

Arnie Lightning Books

Copyright © 2016 by Hey Sup Bye Publishing

All rights reserved. This book is a work of fiction. Graphics used in this book are licensed and © Dollar Photo Club. No part of this book or this book as a whole may be used, reproduced, or transmitted in any form or means without written permission from the publisher.

ISBN-13: 978-1535025904
ISBN-10: 1535025905

"A day without laughter is a day wasted."

–Charlie Chaplin

CONTENTS

FREE GIFT 1

FUNNY BEE JOKES 3

FIND THE DIFFERENCES #1 19

FIND THE DIFFERENCES #2 20

MAZE #1 21

MAZE #2 22

MAZE #3 23

MAZE #4 24

SOLUTIONS 25

ABOUT THE AUTHOR 29

FREE GIFT

 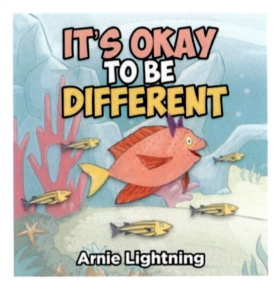

"It's Okay to Be Different" is a beautifully illustrated story about accepting and celebrating others for their differences. It's a great way to teach children to appreciate and accept others for who they are.

To claim your FREE GIFT, simply go to www.ArnieLightning.com/freegift and enter your email address. Shortly thereafter, I will send you a free eBook for you to enjoy!

Please visit: www.ArnieLightning.com/freegift

FUNNY BEE JOKES

Q: What are the smartest bees?

A: Spelling bees!

Q: Can bees fly in the rain?

A: Not without their little yellow jackets!

Q: What did the bee say to the flower?

A: Hello honey!

Q: What do bees chew?

A: Bumble gum!

Q: What does the Santa Claus Bee say?

A: Ho hum hum!

Q: Why do bees have sticky hair?

A: Because the use honey combs!

Q: Why did the bees go on strike?

A: Because they wanted more honey and shorter working flowers!

Q: What TV station do bees watch the most?

A: Bee Bee C (BBC)!

Q: How many bees do you need in a bee choir?

A: One humdred!

Q: What is a bee's favorite novel?

A: The Great Gats-bee!

Q: Who is the bee's favorite singer?

A: Sting!

Q: Who is the bee's favorite pop group?

A: The bee gees!

Q: Where do bees keep their money?

A: In a honey box!

Q: What did the bee say to the other bee in summer?

A: Swarm in here, don't you think?

Q: What does a bee get at McDonalds?

A: A humburger!

Q: Why do bees buzz?

A: Because they cannot whistle!

Q: What is the bee's favorite film?

A: The Sting!

Q: What is a baby bee?

A: A little humbug!

Q: Who is a bee's favorite painter?

A: Pablo Beecasso!

Q: What bee is good for your health?

A: Vitamin bee!

Q: What is black and yellow and buzzes along at 25,000 feet?

A: A bee is an airplane!

Q: What do you call a bee that has a spell put on him?

A: Bee-witched!

Q: What do bees do if they want to use public transport?

A: Wait at the buzz stop!

Q: What is a bee-line?

A: The shortest distance between two buzz-stops!

Q: What do bees wear to work?

A: Buzzness suits!

Q: What goes hum-choo, hum-choo?

A: A bee with a cold!

Q: What do you get when you cross a bell with a bee?

A: A humdinger!

Q: What is a bee's favorite classical music composer?

A: Bee-thoven!

Q: What does a queen bee do when she burps?

A: Issues a royal pardon!

Q: Who writes books for little bees?

A: Bee-trix Potter!

Q: What is black, yellow, and covered in blackberries?

A: A bramble bee!

Q: What is more dangerous than being with a fool?

A: Fooling with a bee!

Q: What do you get from a bee that has an udder?

A: Milk and honey!

Q: Why did the bee start talking poetry?

A: He was waxing lyrical!

Q: What did the bee say to the naughty bee?

A: Bee-hive yourself!

Q: What does a bee say before it stings you?

A: This is going to hurt me a lot more than it is going to hurt you!

Q: How does a queen bee get around her hive?

A: She is throne!

Q: What kind of bee can keep an aero plane dry?

A: An aero-drone!

Q: Where do bees go on vacation?

A: Stingapore!

Q: What is black and yellow, buzzes, and goes along the bottom of the sea?

A: A bee in a submarine!

Q: Why did the queen bee kick out all of the other bees?

A: Because they kept droning on and on!

Q: What kind of bee is hard to understand?

A: A mumble bee!

Q: What goes zzub, zzub?

A: A bee flying backwards!

Q: Why do bees hum?

A: They do not know the words!

Q: What is a bee's favorite flower?

A: Bee-gonias!

Q: What did the confused bee say?

A: To bee or not to bee?

Q: What kinds of bees hum and drop things?

A: A fumble bee!

FIND THE DIFFERENCES #1

FIND 10 DIFFERENCES

FIND THE DIFFERENCES #2

FIND
10
DIFFERENCES

MAZE #1

MAZE #2

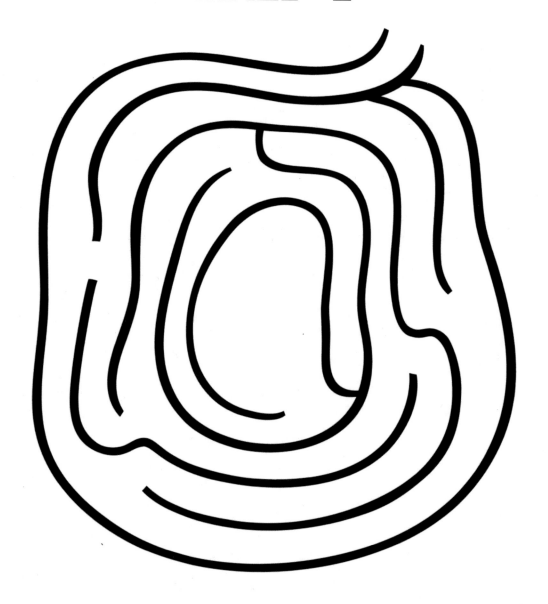

MAZE #3

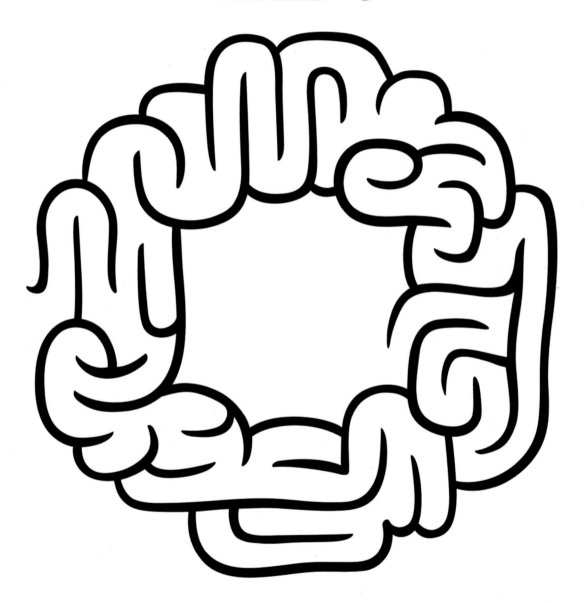

MAZE #4

SOLUTIONS

FIND **10** DIFFERENCES

FIND **10** DIFFERENCES

ABOUT THE AUTHOR

Arnie Lightning is a dreamer. He believes that everyone should dream big and not be afraid to take chances to make their dreams come true. Arnie enjoys writing, reading, doodling, and traveling. In his free time, he likes to play video games and run. Arnie lives in Mississippi where he graduated from The University of Southern Mississippi in Hattiesburg, MS.

For more books by Arnie Lightning please visit:
www.ArnieLightning.com/books